FOR ROBERT

WITH LOVE FROM

DENISE & KEN

Presentation Page

A gift for: _____

From: _____

The
God
Memorandum

Other Books by OG MANDINO

The Greatest
Salesman In The World

The Greatest
Secret In The World

The Greatest
Miracle In The World

These books of enduring value are
published by Fell Publishers, Inc.
Hollywood, Florida

The God Memorandum

from

The Greatest Miracle in the World

by
Og Mandino

FELL PUBLISHERS, INC.
Hollywood, Florida

Over 2,500,000 copies in print, including French, Spanish, Japanese and Portuguese

This publication is designed to provide accurate and authoritative information in regard to the subject matter covered. It is sold with the understanding that the publisher is not engaged in rendering legal, accounting, or other professional service. If legal advice or other assistance is required, the services of a competent professional person should be sought. *From a Declaration of Principles jointly adopted by a Committee of the American Bar Association and a Committee of Publishers.*

Library of Congress Cataloging-in-Publication Data

Mandino, Og
    The God memorandum: from the greatest miracle in the world / by Og Mandino.
        p.   cm.
    ISBN   0-8119-0657-4
    1. Success. 2. Happiness. 3. Conduct of life. I. Title.
    BJ611.2.M317   1993
    170'.44--dc20
                         90-46085
                         CIP

The text of *The God Momorandum* itself first appeared in *The Greatest Miracle in the World*, by Og Mandino copyright 1975, published by Frederick Fell Publishers, Inc.

Fourth Edition

Contents

The
God
Memorandum

Testimonials

Dear Reader:

Literally not a day goes by that I do not receive a letter from a reader somewhere relating how *The God Memorandum** has changed his life. I would like to share with you some of these comments, so that you too will learn how Og Mandino's message has inspired, influenced, and changed the lives of millions of people, and can change yours too.

---

*which originally was published in *The Greatest Miracle in the World*.

"This is the most moving book I have ever read. It is loaded with the facts of life, and a message that we all need. The hand of God has most assuredly touched this work."

W.P.
Roswell, N.M.

"When I read The God Memorandum...*I finally realized I just found my best friend."*

B.S.
North Highlands, Ca.

"I felt the whole book was written just for me. I was so moved and touched by it, and already I feel the impression it has made on my mind...a very moving experience."

E.M.
Edmonton, Canada

"The God Memorandum is an excellent base for renewing self-esteem and national pride. It is what everyone needs to begin cleaning up their mental environment, to create positive thought patterns."

D.E.
Seattle, Wash.

"I sat in the solitude of my office and felt your story; I cried, I smiled. Thank you so much for The God Memorandum.*"*

> J.G.
> Salt Lake City, Utah

"I would like you to know that The God Memorandum *has become my bedside companion."*

> G.S.
> San Francisco, Ca.

"Last July I tried to commit suicide, and like a fool I gave up on life. A few days afterwards I received your book as a birthday gift. I must say it was the best gift I could have received. I was tired of just existing, and I'm fairly young. I'm living now to my fullest, and very happily, too. Your book has opened me up to a new world and outlook on life."

> P.V.L.
> Orlando, Fla.

"The God Memorandum *opened my eyes to all
the potential that lies within me. I have marked my
calendar. The hundredth day falls on April 26th,
which is also my mother's birthday. What a won-
derful present I will have ready to give her this
year—her daughter!"*

J.H.
New York, N.Y.

"*I have had many doubts about myself in the last
few years, and your message has inspired me more
than anything else ever has. Og, I needed your book!
It has moved me!"*

D.F.
East Point, Ga.

"*I believe that if anything could act to change my
life, this book can!"*

R.B.
Menard, Ill.

"*I can't express in words the meaning* The God
Memorandum *has for me. To put into words a few
of my feelings about the single 'positive' outlook on
life.*"

J.T.
Chevy Chase, Md.

"Every night when I read The God Memorandum *I get something different out of it. It gets better every time I read it. I was one of those people who needed to be picked up from the rag pile of life. I think I am returning to humanity from a 'living death'. God bless you."*

> P.P.
> Solon, Ohio

"I must have my own copy of The God Memorandum. *I loved every word. I must read it every day. It thrills my soul. I would that I could put one in the hands of every living person on earth."*

> C.N.
> Reno, Nev.

"I read your book, Mr. Mandino. It changed my life. In all my years of reading anything and everything I could get my hands on, I have never come across a written work of art that so completely moved me. I was in tears halfway through The God Memorandum. *I have faithfully read it each and every night since November 17th, and have purchased a few copies for my friends this Christmas."*

> R.J.A.
> Las Vegas, Nev.

"Just a short note to let you know I am still faithfully reading The God Memorandum *nightly. Today marks one month into the project, and I have to admit that certain noticeable changes are beginning to take place."*

> B.S.
> Chico, Ca.

"I spent the whole evening last night reading your book, and could not put it down. Never in my life have I been so inspired by a book or enjoyed it as much as this one. I was left with the greatest feeling I have ever experienced. The God Memorandum really makes you stop and think how lucky you really are."

> R.M.W.
> Pittsburgh, Pa.

And following is a selection of comments we have received from well-known people who have been touched by Og Mandino's motivating book:

"Today when millions of people are troubled, uncertain and confused, Og Mandino has the answer. There never was a time when millions of people were more desperately in need of faith, hope and courage and peace of mind, of standards and ideals by which to live and above all an abiding belief in the future and in the progress of mankind."

> Lester J. Bradshaw, Jr.
> President,
> Bradshaw
> Associates, Inc.

"The book is another great...exciting, captivating, and motivating. Read and Believe."

> Richard M. DeVos,
> President,
> Amway Corporation

"This could be literally a Godsend to millions of young and old who desperately need this message. From time to time, everyone needs a memorandum from God to remind us of The Greatest Miracle in the World. This inspirational book belongs in everyone's library."

Dr. Jaye B. Marchant
President,
Marchant Investors, Inc.

"Og Mandino has done it again! He has written another book which will rival his classic best seller, The Greatest Salesman in the World."

Harlan Smith
Vice President
Kroch's and Brentano's

"I am delighted with Og Mandino's latest book...here again, one of the greatest inspirational writers of our time has produced a work that will lift the mind and heart of every reader with powerful motivational appeal...It will produce miracles in the lives of thousands of people."

Norman Vincent Peale

"A super book that will kindle the pilot light of all those who desire to become professional rag pickers, as well as those who need to be picked up from the rag pile of life."

Rick Forzano
(Former) Head Coach,
Detroit Lions

"About this book: if you are thinking about buying a copy, don't buy one. Buy several. You will definitely want them for your friends who will love it as much as you."

Dr. Marcus Bach

"It's spring again. Og Mandino is back. As we cattlemen say, 'He wintered real good.' He returns from hibernation with another means of inspiring each of us to be something more than we are."

Paul Harvey
Paul Harvey News
American
Broadcasting Company

"Last night I started the one-hundred-day treatment complete with cloth and pin. Thank you for a great book of inspiration and...I will be placing copies in a great many needy places."

Reverend
Raymond Buckley
Pastor,
Highland Park Church
of the Nazarene
Seattle, Wash.

"I say with all honesty that this is the most fulfilling piece of work I have ever read...I have been moved like never before...Og, please keep this kind of work coming...The world needs you."

Ralph W. Gabbard
Vice President,
WKYT-TV
Lexington, Ky.

A Special Message
from the Publisher

Dearest Reader,

The God Memorandum is truly a masterpiece. In all my years as a publisher, I've never seen such inspiration.

It will soothe your spirit with beauty and peace; yet, the author's message will entice you to live boldly with newfound vision.

The author, Og Mandino, will uplift you and help you turn disastrous problems into trivial obstacles.

Inner peace is the goal — and it's Og Mandino's gift to you.

It was a privilege to read and an honor to publish *The God Memorandum*. May it touch your heart as it has mine.

Most cordially,

Donald L. Lessne
Publisher

A Special Message
from the Author

I feel toward *The God Memorandum* the same deep emotions of love and pride that any parent experiences when his or her child goes out into the world and achieves success, fame, and acclamation.

Were I a stamp collector I could have already filled several worldwide albums with lovely philatelic designs removed from envelopes bearing letters to me from all parts of our globe...letters spelling out in graphic details the amazing changes that have taken place in the lives of those who used *The God Memorandum* exactly as instructed.

What exactly do you want from life?

What exactly would you like for your family that you have not been able to give them, caught up as you are with the rest of us in this eternal struggle for mere survival?

If you can answer the above two questions honestly and specifically, then *The God Memorandum* can help you achieve your goals...no matter how hopeless and out of reach they may seem to you at this moment.

Let me warn you, before we go any further, that you are going to have to pay a price...but it's really quite small when compared to the benefits you are going to reap. Reading *The God Memorandum* but once and then putting it aside will do little toward moving you toward your goals. After all, and be honest, you didn't get into the position you are in now overnight, and so you must not expect to be sitting on top of golden pyramids within twenty-four hours either.

Everything in life worth having is worth working for...whether it be endless hours of practice to improve your golf swing, tennis stroke, or pitching control or weeks, months, and years of concentrated study and application in order to advance your career. Happily, for those of us with even a small spark of ambition, we live in a world where "there ain't no free lunch" and those who expect one will be lost forever in the crowd of mediocrity.

So what do I expect from you? What kind of "price" must you pay in order to become the person you know you can be?

I want twenty minutes of your
time, each day, for the next
one hundred days!

Not a very high price, is it? I'm sure that you, like the rest of us, waste many more minutes than that each day. Therefore I'm not asking you for anything that is not in your power to give.

And what do I want you to do with those twenty minutes? Simple. Just before you go to sleep each night, read *The God Memorandum*. All of it. If you are going to begin now, then circle today's date on your calendar. Count ahead one hundred days and circle that date. Read the entire *Memorandum* every night until you get to the second circle. That's all!

Approach *The God Memorandum* with an open heart. Faith that it will work isn't necessary at first. That will come to you as the days progress. For now, just tell yourself that you've got nothing to lose by trying it...and much to gain if this guy Mandino is really leveling with you.

Each night, after you have completed your reading, sleep in peace while the message you have read gradually seeps down into your deep, subconscious mind, which never sleeps. Gradually, as your new program for success and happiness becomes imprinted on your inner being, you will notice great changes in yourself, as will those around you.

By the hundredth day you will be a new person...a living miracle...resurrected from a life that once seemed to be headed nowhere. Then you must take one more step. Find someone who, like your old self, seems to be spinning his or her wheels. Give that person a copy of *The God Memorandum*. Share your good fortune.

Later, if you would like to learn the origin of *The God Memorandum*, you might wish to get yourself a copy of the book from whence it came, *The Greatest Miracle in the World*. Then you will truly understand how your life has been changed through your own efforts, how you have become the new you.

Now begin...and let nothing prevent you from completing your hundred days.

You give me twenty minutes a day, and I'll return to you a human being you'll be proud to see in your mirror. That's an offer you just can't refuse.

OG MANDINO
Scottsdale, Arizona

Instructions from
Simon Potter*
through Og Mandino

The God Memorandum is now in your possession and it is my desire that you share it, eventually, with the world, but only after you apply its principles to your own life, consonant with my instructions.

Remember that the most difficult tasks are consummated, not by a single explosive burst of energy or effort, but by consistent daily application of the best you have within you.

To change one's life for the better, to ressurrect one's body and mind from living

---

*For the complete inspirational story of Simon Potter the Ragpicker, read *The Greatest Miracle in the World,* by Og Mandino, published by Fell Publishers, Inc., 2131 Hollywood Boulevard, Hollywood, FL 33020.

death, requires many positive steps, one in front of the other, with your sights always on your goal.

The God Memorandum is only your ticket to a new life. It will do nothing for you unless you open your mind and your heart to receive it. By itself it will move you not one inch in any direction. The means of transportation, and the power to break your inertia, must be generated by forces long dormant but still alive within you. Follow these rules and your forces will self-ignite.

1. First, mark this day upon your calendar.* Then, count forward one hundred days and mark that day. This will establish the length of your mission without the necessity of your counting each day as you live it.

---

*A special hundred days' calendar for your personal use follows this message.

2. Next, become aware of a small
   safety pin to which has been
   attached a tiny piece of white rag
   in the shape of a square. This
   combination of pin and rag, two
   of the most common and
   unprepossessing materials in the
   world, is your ragpicker's secret
   amulet.

   Wear your amulet on your
   person in a place visible to you as
   a constant reminder during the
   next hundred days that you are
   trying to live as you are being
   instructed to live in *The God
   Memorandum*. Your pin and rag
   are symbols...a sign that you are
   in the process of changing your
   life from the pins and rags of
   failure to the treasures of a new
   and better life.

3. Do not, under any conditions, divulge the meaning of your amulet to those who may inquire during your hundred-day mission.

4. Read *The God Memorandum* before your retire, each night, for one hundred nights...and then sleep in peace, while the message you have read gradually seeps down into your deep mind that never sleeps. Let no reason or excuse force you to forego the reading for even one night.

Gradually, as the days become weeks, you will notice great changes in yourself...as will those around you. By the hundredth day...you will be a living miracle..a new person...filled with beauty and wonder and ambition and ability.

Then, and only then, find someone who,

like your old self, needs help. Give him two things: your ragpicker's secret amulet... and *The God Memorandum*.

And one more thing give to him...as I have given to you...love.

I have a vision wherein I can see thousands upon thousands wearing our ragpicker's amulets. People will encounter each other in the marketplace, on the street, in their places of worship, in their public conveyances, in their schools, and on their job and they will look upon each other's insignificant pin and rag and smile at their brothers and sisters...for each will know that the other is embarked on the same mission, the same dream, with a common purpose...to change their own life for the better and thus, joined together, change their world.

With love,
Simon

Your Hundred Days' Calendar

	Month	Date	Year
Day 1			

Circle each day as you complete your reading

1	2	3	4	5	6	7	8	9	10
11	12	13	14	15	16	17	18	19	20
21	22	23	24	25	26	27	28	29	30
31	32	33	34	35	36	37	38	39	40
41	42	43	44	45	46	47	48	49	50
51	52	53	54	55	56	57	58	59	60
61	62	63	64	65	66	67	68	69	70
71	72	73	74	75	76	77	78	79	80
81	82	83	84	85	86	87	88	89	90
91	92	93	94	95	96	97	98	99	100

	Month	Date	Year
Day 100			

The
God
Memorandum

To You
From God

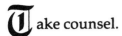ake counsel.

I hear your cry.

It passes through the darkness, filters through the clouds, mingles with starlight, and finds its way to my heart on the path of a sunbeam.

I have anguished over the cry of a hare choked in the noose of a snare, a sparrow tumbled from the nest of its mother, a child thrashing helplessly in a pond, and a son shedding his blood on a cross.

Know that I hear you, also. Be at peace. Be calm.

J bring thee relief for your sorrow for I know its cause...and its cure.

𝔜ou weep for all your childhood dreams that have vanished with the years.

You weep for all your self-esteem that has been corrupted by failure.

You weep for all your potential that has been bartered for security.

You weep for all your individuality that has been trampled by mobs.

You weep for all your talent that has been wasted through misuse.

𝔜ou look upon yourself with disgrace and you turn in terror from the image you see in the pool. Who is this mockery of humanity staring back at you with bloodless eyes of shame?

Where is the grace of your manner, the beauty of your figure, the quickness of your movement, the clarity of your mind, the brilliance of your tongue? Who stole your goods. Is the thief's identity known to you, as it is to me?

Once you placed your head in a pillow of grass in your father's field and looked up at a cathedral of clouds and knew that all the gold of Babylon would be yours in time.

Once you read from many books and wrote on many tablets, convinced beyond any doubt that all the wisdom of Solomon would be equaled and surpassed by you.

And the seasons would flow into years

until lo, you would reign supreme in your own garden of Eden.

𝕯ost thou remember who implanted those plans and dreams and seeds of hope within you?

You cannot.

You have no memory of that moment when first you emerged from your mother's womb and I placed my hand on your soft brow. And the secret I whispered in your small ear when I bestowed my blessings upon you?

Remember our secret?

You cannot.

𝕿he passing years have destroyed your

recollection, for they have filled your mind with fear and doubt and anxiety and remorse and hate and there is no room for joyful memories where these beasts habitate.

Weep no more, I am with you...and this moment is the dividing line of your life. All that has gone before is like unto no more than that time you slept within your mother's womb. What is past is dead. Let the dead bury the dead.

This day you return from the living dead.

This day, like unto Elijah with the widow's son, I stretch myself upon thee three times and you live again.

This day, like unto Elisha with thee

Shunammite's son, I put my mouth upon your mouth and my eyes upon your eyes and my hands upon your hands and your flesh is warm again.

This day, like unto Jesus at the tomb of Lazarus, I command you to come forth and you will walk from your cave of doom to begin a new life.

This is your birthday. This is your new date of birth. Your first life, like unto a play of the theatre, was only a rehearsal. This time the curtain is up. This time the world watches and waits to applaud. This time you will not fail.

Light your candles. Share your cake. Pour the wine. You have been reborn.

Like a butterfly from its chrysalis you will fly...fly as high as you wish, and neither the wasps nor dragonflies nor mantids of mankind shall obstruct your mission or your search for the true riches of life.

Feel my hand upon thy head.

Attend to my wisdom.

Let me share with you, again, the secret you heard at your birth and forgot.

You are my greatest miracle.

You are the greatest miracle in the world.

Those were the first words you ever heard. Then you cried. They all cry.

You did not believe me then...and nothing has happened in the intervening years to correct your disbelief. For how could you be a miracle when you consider yourself a failure at the most menial of tasks? How can you be a miracle when you have little confidence in dealing with the most trivial of responsibilities? How can you be a miracle when you are shackled by debt and lie awake in torment over whence will come tomorrow's bread?

Enough. The milk that is spilled is sour. Yet, how many prophets, how many wise men, how many poets, how many artists, how many composers, how many scientists, how many philosophers and messengers have I sent with the word of your divinity, your potential for godli-

ness, and the secrets of achievement?
How did you treat them?

Still I love you and I am with you now,
through these words, to fulfill the
prophet who announced that the Lord
shall set his hand again, the second time,
to recover the remnant of his people.

I have set my hand again.

This is the second time.

You are my remnant.

It is of no avail to ask, haven't you
known, haven't you heard, hasn't it been
told to you from the beginning; haven't
you understood from the foundations of
the earth?

You have not known; you have not heard; you have not understood.

You have been told that you are a divinity in disguise, a god playing fool.

You have been told that you are a special piece of work, noble in reason, infinite in faculties, express and admirable in form and moving, like an angel in action, like a god in apprehension.

You have been told that you are the salt of the earth.

You were given the secret even of moving mountains, of performing the impossible.

You believed no one. You burned your map to happiness, you abandoned your claim to peace of mind, you snuffed out the candles that had been placed along your destined path of glory, and then you stumbled, lost and frightened, in the darkness of futility and self-pity, until you fell into a hell of your own creation.

Then you cried and beat your breast and cursed the luck that had befallen you. You refused to accept the consequences of your own petty thoughts and lazy deeds and you searched for a scapegoat on which to blame your failure. How quickly you found one.

You blamed me!

You cried that your handicaps, your

mediocrity, your lack of opportunity, your failures...were the will of God!

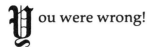ou were wrong!

Let us take inventory. Let us, first, call a roll of your handicaps. For how can I ask you to build a new life lest you have the tools?

Are you blind? Does the sun rise and fall without your witness?

No. You can see...and the hundred million receptors I have placed in your eyes enable you to enjoy the magic of a leaf, a snowflake, a pond, an eagle, a child, a cloud, a star, a rose, a rainbow...and the look of love. Count one blessing.

Are you deaf? Can a baby laugh or cry without your attention?

No. You can hear...and the twenty-four thousand fibers I have built in each of your ears vibrate to the wind in the trees, the tides on the rocks, the majesty of an opera, a robin's plea, children at play...and the words "I love you." Count another blessing.

Are you mute? Do your lips move and bring forth only spittle?

No. You can speak...as can no other of my creatures, and your words can calm the angry, uplift the despondent, goad the quitter, cheer the unhappy, warm the lonely, praise the worthy, encourage the defeated, teach the ignorant...and say I love you. Count another blessing.

Are you paralyzed? Does your helpless form despoil the land?

No. You can move. You are not a tree condemned to a small plot while the wind and world abuse you. You can stretch and run and dance and work, for within you I have designed five hundred muscles, two hundred bones, and seven miles of nerve fibre all synchronized by me to do your bidding. Count another blessing.

Are you unloved and unloving? Does loneliness engulf you, night and day?

No. No more. For now you know love's secret, that to receive love it must be given with no thought of its return. To love for fulfillment, satisfaction, or pride, is no love. Love is a gift on which no return is demanded. Now you know that to love unselfishly is its own reward. And even should love not be returned it is not lost, for love not reciprocated will flow back to you and soften and purify your heart. Count another blessing. Count twice.

Is your heart stricken? Does it leak and strain to maintain your life?

No. Your heart is strong. Touch your chest and feel its rhythm, pulsating, hour after hour, day and night, thirty-six million beats each year, year after year, asleep or awake, pumping your blood through more than sixty thousand miles of veins, arteries, and tubing...pumping more than six hundred thousand gallons each year. Man has never created such a machine. Count another blessing.

Are you diseased of skin? Do people turn in horror when you approach?

No. Your skin is clear and a marvel of creation, needing only that you tend it with soap and oil and brush and care. In time all steels will tarnish and rust, but not your skin. Eventually the strongest of metals will wear, with use, but not that layer that I have constructed around you. Constantly it renews itself, old cells replaced by new, just as the old you is now being replaced by the new. Count another blessing.

Are your lungs befouled? Does the breath of life struggle to enter your body?

No. Your portholes to life support you even in the vilest of environments of your own making, and they labor always to filter life-giving oxygen through six hundred million pockets of folded flesh while they rid your body of gaseous wastes. Count another blessing.

𝕴s your blood poisoned? Is it diluted with water and pus?

No. Within your five quarts of blood are twenty-two trillion blood cells and within each cell are millions of molecules and within each molecule is an atom oscillating at more than ten million times each second. Each second, two million of your blood cells die to be replaced by two million more in a resurrection that has continued since your first birth. As it has always been inside, so now it is on your outside. Count another blessing.

re you feeble of mind? Can you no longer think for yourself?

No. Your brain is the most complex structure in the universe. I know. Within its three pounds are fifteen billion nerve cells, more than three times as many cells as there are people on your earth. To help you file away every perception, every sound, every taste, every smell, every action you have experienced since the day of your birth, I have implanted within your cells, more than one thousand billion billion protein molecules. Every incident in your life is there waiting only your recall. And, to assist your brain in the control of your body I have dispersed, throughout your form, four million pain-sensitive structures, five hundred thousand touch detectors, and more than two hundred thousand temperature detectors. No nation's gold is better protected than you. None of your ancient wonders are greater than you.

ᵓou are my finest creation.

ᵚithin you is enough atomic energy to destroy any of the world's great cities...and rebuild it.

Are you poor? Is there no gold or silver in your purse?

No. You are rich! Together we have just counted your wealth. Study the list. Count them again. Tally your assets!

Why have you betrayed yourself? Why have you cried that all the blessings of humanity were removed from you? Why did you deceive yourself that you were powerless to change your life? Are you without talent, senses, abilities, pleasures, instincts, sensations, and pride? Are you without hope? Why do you cringe in the shadows, a giant defeated, awaiting only sympathetic transport into the welcome void and dampness of hell?

You have so much. Your blessings overflow your cup...and you have been unmindful of them, like a child spoiled in luxury, since I have bestowed them upon you with generosity and regularity.

Answer me.

Answer yourself.

What rich man, old and sick, feeble and helpless, would not exchange all the gold in his vault for the blessings you have treated so lightly?

Know then the first secret to happiness and success you possess, even now, every blessing necessary to achieve great glory. They are your treasure, your tools with which to build, starting today, the foundation for a new and better life.

Therefore, I say unto you, count your blessings and know that you already are my greatest creation. This is the first law you must obey in order to perform the greatest miracle in the world, the return of your humanity from living death.

And be grateful for your lessons learned in poverty. For he is not poor who has little; only he that desires much...and true security lies not in the things one has but in the things one can do without.

Where are the handicaps that produced your failure? They existed only in your mind.

Count your blessings.

And the second law is like unto the first. Proclaim your rarity.

You had condemned yourself to a potter's field, and there you lay, unable to forgive your own failure, destroying yourself with self-hate, self-incrimination, and revulsion at your crimes against yourself and others.

Are you not perplexed?

Do you not wonder why I am able to forgive your failures, your transgressions, your pitiful demeanor...when you cannot forgive yourself?

I address you now, for three reasons. You need me. You are not one of a herd heading for destruction in a gray mass of mediocrity. And...you are a great rarity.

Consider a painting by Rembrandt or a bronze by Degas or a violin by Stradivarius or a play by Shakespeare. They have great value for two reasons: their creators were masters and they are few in number. Yet there are more than one of each of these.

On that reasoning you are the most valuable treasure on the face of the earth, for you know who created you and there is only one of you.

Never, in all the seventy billion humans who have walked this planet since the beginning of time has there been anyone exactly like you.

Never, until the end of time, will there be another such as you.

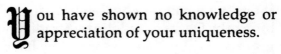

ou have shown no knowledge or appreciation of your uniqueness.

Yet, you are the rarest thing in the world.

From your father, in his moment of supreme love, flowed countless seeds of love, more than four hundred million in number. All of them, as they swam within your mother, gave up the ghost and died. All except one! You.

You alone persevered within the loving warmth of your mother's body, searching for your other half, a single cell from your mother so small that more than two million would be necessary to fill an acorn shell. Yet, despite impossible odds, in that vast ocean of darkness and disaster, you persevered, found that infinitesimal cell, joined with it, and began a new life. Your life.

𝔜ou arrived, bringing with you, as does every child, the message that I was not yet discouraged of man. Two cells, now united in a miracle. Two cells, each containing twenty-three chromosomes and within each chromosome hundreds of genes, which would govern every characteristic about you, from the color of your eyes to the charm of your manner to the size of your brain.

𝔚ith all the combinations at my command, beginning with that single sperm from your father's four hundred million, through the hundreds of genes in each of the chromosomes from your mother and father, I could have created three hundred thousand billion humans, each different from the other.

But who did I bring forth?

You! One of a kind. Rarest of the rare. A priceless treasure, possessed of qualities in mind and speech and movement and appearance and actions as no other who has ever lived, lives, or shall live.

Why have you valued yourself in pennies when you are worth a king's ransom?

Why did you listen to those who demeaned you...and far worse, why did you believe them?

𝕿ake counsel. No longer hide your rarity in the dark. Bring it forth. Show the world. Strive not to walk as your brother walks, nor talk as your leader talks, nor labor as do the mediocre. Never do as another. Never imitate. For how do you know that you may not imitate evil; and he who imitates evil always goes beyond the example set, while he who imitates what is good always falls short. Imitate no one. Be yourself. Show your rarity to the world and they will shower you with gold. This then is the second law.

𝕻roclaim your rarity.

And now you have received two laws.

Count your blessings! Proclaim your rarity!

You have no handicaps. You are not mediocre.

You nod. You force a smile. You admit your self-deception.

What of your next complaint? Opportunity never seeks thee!

Take counsel and it shall come to pass, for now I give you the law of success in every venture. Many centuries ago this law was given to your forefathers from a mountain top. Some heeded the law and lo, their life was filled with the fruit of happiness, accomplishment, gold, and peace of mind. Most listened not, for they sought magic means, devious routes, or waited for the devil called luck to deliver to them the riches of life. They waited in vain...just as you waited, and then they wept, as you wept, blaming their lack of fortune on my will.

The law is simple. Young or old, pauper or king, white or black, male or female...all can use the secret to their advantage; for of all the rules and speeches and scriptures of success and how to attain it, only one method has never failed...whomsoever shall compel ye to go with him one mile...go with him two.

This then is the third law...the secret that will produce riches and acclaim beyond your dreams. Go another mile!

The only certain means of success is to render more and better service than is expected of you, no matter what your task may be. This is a habit followed by all successful people since the beginning of time. Therefore I saith the surest way to doom yourself to mediocrity is to perform only the work for which you are paid.

Think not ye are being cheated if you deliver more than the silver you receive. For there is a pendulum to all life and the sweat you deliver, if not rewarded today, will swing back tomorrow, tenfold. The mediocre never goes another mile, for why should he cheat himself, he thinks. But you are not mediocre. To go another mile is a privilege you must appropriate by your own initiative. You cannot, you must not avoid it. Neglect it, do only as little as the others, and the responsibility for your failure is yours alone.

You can no more render service without receiving just compensation than you can withhold the rendering of it without suffering the loss of reward. Cause and effect, means and ends, seed and fruit, these cannot be separated. The effect already blooms in the cause, the end preexists in the means, and the fruit is always in the seed.

Go another mile.

Concern yourself not, should you serve an ungrateful master. Serve him more.

And instead of him, let it be me who is in your debt, for then you will know that every minute, every stroke of extra service will be repaid. And worry not, should your reward not come soon. For the longer payment is withheld, the better for you...and compound interest on compound interest is the law's greatest benefit.

You cannot command success, you can only deserve it...and now you know the great secret necessary in order to merit its rare reward.

Go another mile!

Where is this field from whence you cried there was no opportunity? Look! Look around thee. See, where only yesterday you wallowed on the refuse of self-pity, you now walk tall on a carpet of gold. Nothing has changed...except you, but you are everything.

You are my greatest miracle.

You are the greatest miracle in the world.

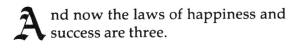nd now the laws of happiness and success are three.

Count your blessings! Proclaim your rarity! Go another mile!

Be patient with your progress. To count your blessings with gratitude, to proclaim your rarity with pride, to go an extra mile and then another, these acts are not accomplished in the blinking of an eye. Yet, that which you acquire with most difficulty you retain the longest; as those who have earned a fortune are more careful of it than those by whom it was inherited.

And fear not as you enter your new life. Every noble acquisition is attended with its risks. He who fears to encounter the one must not expect to obtain the other. Now you know you are a miracle. And there is no fear in a miracle.

Be proud. You are not the momentary whim of a careless creator experimenting in the laboratory of life. You are not a slave of forces that you cannot comprehend. You are a free manifestation of no force but mine, of no love but mine. You were made with a purpose.

Feel my hand. Hear my words.

You need me...and I need you.

We have a world to rebuild...and if it requireth a miracle what is that to us? We are both miracles and now we have each other.

Never have I lost faith in you since that day when I first spun you from a giant wave and tossed you helplessly on the sands. As you measure time that was more than five hundred million years ago. There were many models, many shapes, many sizes, before I reached perfection in you more than thirty thousand years ago. I have made no further effort to improve on you in all these years.

For how could one improve on a miracle? You were a marvel to behold and I was pleased. I gave you this world and dominion over it. Then, to enable you to reach your full potential I placed my hand upon you, once more, and endowed you with powers unknown to any other creature in the universe, even unto this day.

𝕵 gave you the power to think.

I gave you the power to love.

I gave you the power to will.

I gave you the power to laugh.

I gave you the power to imagine.

I gave you the power to create.

I gave you the power to plan.

I gave you the power to speak.

𝕵 gave you the power to pray.

My pride in you knew no bounds. You were my ultimate creation, my greatest miracle. A complete living being. One who can adjust to any climate, any hardship, any challenge. One who can manage his own destiny without interference from me. One who can translate a sensation or perception, not by instinct, but by thought and deliberation into whatever action is best for himself and all humanity.

Thus we come to the fourth law of success and happiness...for I gave you one more power, a power so great that not even my angels possess it.

I gave you...the power to choose.

With this gift I placed you even above my angels...for angels are not free to choose sin. I gave you complete control over your destiny. I told you to determine, for yourself, your own nature in accordance with your own free will. Neither heavenly nor earthly in nature, you were free to fashion yourself in whatever form you preferred. You had the power to choose to degenerate into the lowest forms of life, but you also had the power, out of your soul's judgement, to be reborn into the higher forms, which are divine.

𝕴 have never withdrawn your great power, the power to choose.

What have you done with this tremendous force? Look at yourself. Think of the choices you have made in your life and recall, now, those bitter moments when you would fall to your knees if only you had the opportunity to choose again.

What is past is past...and now you know the fourth great law of happiness and success...Use wisely, your power of choice.

ℭhoose to love...rather than hate.

Choose to laugh...rather than cry.

Choose to create...rather than destroy.

Choose to persevere...rather than quit.

Choose to praise...rather than gossip.

Choose to heal...rather than wound.

Choose to give...rather than steal.

Choose to act...rather than procrastinate.

Choose to grow...rather than rot.

Choose to pray...rather than curse.

Choose to live...rather than die.

Now you know that your misfortunes were not my will, for all power was vested in you, and the accumulation of deeds and thoughts which placed you on the refuse of humanity were your doing, not mine. My gifts of power were too large for your small nature. Now you have grown tall and wise and the fruits of the land will be yours.

You are more than a human being, you are a human becoming.

You are capable of great wonders. Your potential is unlimited. Who else, among my creatures, has mastered fire? Who else, among my creatures, has conquered gravity, has pierced the heavens, has conquered disease and pestilence and drought?

Never demean yourself again!

Never settle for the crumbs of life!

Never hide your talents, from this day hence!

Remember the child who says "when I am a big boy." But what is that? For the big boy says, "when I grow up." And then grown up, he says, "when I am wed." But to be wed, what is that, after all? The thought then changes to "when I retire." And then, retirement comes, and he looks back over the landscape traversed; a cold wind sweeps over it and somehow he has missed it all and it is gone.

Enjoy this day, today....and tomorrow, tomorrow.

You have performed the greatest miracle in the world.

You have returned from a living death.

You will feel self-pity no more and each new day will be a challenge and a joy.

You have been born again..but just as before, you can choose failure and despair or success and happiness. The choice is yours. The choice is exclusively yours. I can only watch, as before...in pride...or sorrow.

Remember, then, the four laws of happiness and success.

Count your blessings.

Proclaim your rarity.

Go another mile.

Use wisely your power of choice.

And one more, to fulfill the other four. Do all things with love...love for yourself, love for all others, and love for me.

Wipe away your tears. Reach out, grasp my hand, and stand straight.

Let me cut the grave cloths that have bound you.

This day you have been notified.

You are
the Greatest Miracle
in the World

A Note
About the Author

Og Mandino, former president of Success Unlimited, the Chicago-based magazine with a Positive Mental Attitude, is widely acclaimed as one of today's greatest writers of inspirational material.

His articles and short stories have achieved worldwide recognition for their sensitivity and compassion. His books, *The Greatest Salesman in the World, The Greatest Secret in the World,* and *The Greatest Miracle in the World* (all published by Fell), have sold millions of copies in all editions, and have been translated into many languages.

A resident of the Southwest, Mandino is presently devoting all his time to writing and lecturing.